THE POWER OF SPOKEN BLESSINGS

LIFECHANGE BOOKS

BILL GOTHARD

Multnomah Books

THE POWER OF SPOKEN BLESSINGS
published by Multnomah Books
A division of Random House, Inc.
ISBN: 1-59052-375-X

© 2004 by Institute in Basic Life Principles, Inc.

Cover design by The DesignWorks Group
Cover image by Veer

Italics in Scripture quotations are the author's emphasis.
Unless otherwise indicated, Scripture quotations are from:
The Holy Bible, New King James Version © 1984 by Thomas Nelson, Inc.
Other Scripture quotations are from:
The Holy Bible, English Standard Version (ESV)
© 2001 by Crossway Bibles, a division of Good News Publishers.
Used by permission. All rights reserved.
The Amplified Bible (AMP) © 1965, 1987 by Zondervan Publishing House.
The Amplified New Testament © 1958, 1987 by the Lockman Foundation.
Holy Bible, New Living Translation (NLT) © 1996.
Used by permission of Tyndale House Publishers, Inc. All rights reserved.

Multnomah is a trademark of Multnomah Publishers
and is registered in the U.S. Patent and Trademark Office.
The colophon is a trademark of Multnomah Publishers.

For information:
MULTNOMAH BOOKS
12265 ORACLE BOULEVARD, SUITE 200
COLORADO SPRINGS, CO 80921

Library of Congress Cataloging-in-Publication Data

Gothard, Bill.
  The power of spoken blessings / Bill Gothard.
      p. cm. — (Lifechange books)
  Includes bibliographical references.
  ISBN 1-59052-375-X
  1. Benediction. 2. Communication—Religious aspects—Christianity. 3. Faith. I. Title. II. Series.
  BV197.B5G68 2004
  248.3'2—dc22

                                                            2004015755

07 08 09 10—10 9 8 7 6 5 4 3 2 1

Contents

CHAPTER 1

Evidence of Power 5

CHAPTER 2

The Power of a Name 13

CHAPTER 3

The Overlooked Power of Our Words 21

CHAPTER 4

The Power of God's Words 31

CHAPTER 5

Our Model Blessing 43

CHAPTER 6

Blessing Our Children 55

CHAPTER 7

Blessing Our Enemies 67

CHAPTER 8

Blessing God 77

A Testimony 83

Appendix 86

Notes 88

EVIDENCE
OF POWER

After fourteen years, their marriage had hit a flat spot.

It wasn't as though they'd been arguing or fighting or ignoring one another. They were still a deeply devoted couple. And yet…after fourteen years, they had expected and hoped for something more. Where was that higher, deeper level of spiritual bonding between them? It simply wasn't there, and both of them knew it.

So they tried something new.

They began to bless each other—actually speaking aloud words of blessing to one another—at the beginning of each day.

That was more than a quarter-century ago. Today, Bill and Dorothy Jean will tell you that by blessing each other daily, they've developed an extraordinary intimacy of heart, soul, and mind. Their morning discussions are rich and inspiring, and God's power becomes evident to them throughout each day, based on the blessings they gave and received at sunrise.

Offering this kind of spoken blessing to someone is something many of us probably can't quite picture ourselves doing. The situation (as we imagine it) would be awkward at best. Besides, if we decided to try, would we even know how? Just the thought of coming up with the right words is enough of a challenge to hold us back.

But what are the consequences of "holding back"? What might we be missing? What if we could tap into a heavenly reservoir of power, encouragement, and lasting joy—for ourselves, our loved ones, and even for our adversaries?

In fact, we can.

A FIRST BLESSING

At the close of a recent ministry seminar, a teenager came up and asked to speak with me. Under court supervision, she'd had several brushes with the law. I counseled and prayed with her.

Later she wrote me this note:

"You helped me see my need to give God my will, but then you also prayed, and in your prayer you blessed me. That was the first time I had ever been blessed. That blessing has exhorted me to live up to what you said. My life has taken a drastic 180-degree turn! I am amazed by what God actually said in His Word. I have never had understanding like I have now when it comes to reading His Word."

She concluded: "The blessing you gave me started all this, and I don't know how to thank you!"

Our ministry offices receive letter after letter with stories just like this one. Lives, marriages, and whole families are experiencing deepening relationships and spiritual encouragement as we continue to teach the importance of spoken blessings. On an even deeper level, we've been receiving accounts of how spoken blessings have overturned the tormenting memories and oppression of verbal abuse from the past.

A GRANDFATHER'S CURSE

Every time Alicia thought about her grandfather, a violent and painful scene flashed through her mind. Ten years old, she had been trying to comfort her mother, who had been severely burned in a house fire. Her grandfather came into the room and gave Alicia a glare filled with hate and disgust. He walked over to her, jerked her up from the bed, and threw her across the room onto a couch.

Still in shock from this assault, Alicia then felt the lash of his bitter words: "You'll never be good for anything but to be a—" They were words a ten-year-old mind couldn't comprehend, but there was no mistaking the hatred and contempt.

Why would a grandfather spew out such deadly venom toward his ten-year-old granddaughter? Because to him, she represented the shame his daughter had brought upon the family by giving birth out of wedlock. On top of that, Alicia's father was from another ethnic group—a fact that was obvious from the young girl's physical features.

Throughout her childhood and teenage years, Alicia continued to bear the curses of shame from her mother's immorality. Each time she was taunted or ridiculed, her grandfather's painful words blared again in her memory. Tortured with fears of further rejection, anxieties about her future began to consume every waking thought. When she finally married, Alicia brought her emotional turmoil into this new relationship, often finding herself angry and frustrated with her husband and children.

Then one day she learned a way to resolve the pain and rejection of those many past years. It was so simple that she marveled she hadn't learned about it sooner. It amazed her husband, too. He noticed that her tone of voice became more upbeat, and she was no longer harsh with the children.

What did Alicia do? She gave a verbal blessing to that

grandfather who had wounded her so deeply and to the others who had "cursed" her over the years. And just that quickly, the awful pain faded from her heart.

A few days later, Alicia had the opportunity to experience something similar with someone else—this time her husband's father. She and her husband were talking on the phone with him, seeking counsel over a situation in their lives. In the course of the conversation, he responded to their need with unkind words and names, which devastated her. Alicia's hands trembled as she hung up the phone. All the old feelings of hatred and rejection began to well up in her heart again.

Then she remembered her newfound secret. She lifted her hand and gave her father-in-law a spoken blessing. Immediately her trembling stopped, and peace crept back into her troubled heart.

ON THE RECEIVING END

Besides the positive return for those who speak a blessing, many also testify of remarkable effects in the lives of those who receive such words.

A single mother had run out of answers on how to deal with her rebellious teenage son. He tested her patience beyond its limits and, in the process, stirred up negative attitudes in the rest of her children.

She saw no end to the confusion and tension. She tried

to reason with him and asked others to counsel him. She sent him to camps and conferences. But nothing worked.

When she was reminded afresh of the critical need children have to receive praise, she obtained a book that identifies and explains several basic character qualities. Searching through its pages, she couldn't find a single quality that she could honestly say was evident in her son's life. What she did see in the book, however, were many qualities that she believed God wanted to develop within him.

Then she learned about the power of spoken blessings. One day when her children were battling one another again, she interrupted them and said to her combative son, "I want to give you a blessing." He immediately reacted, stating, "I don't want you to bless me." That did not stop her. She recalled some of the qualities that she believed God wanted to cultivate in his life, then said these words in a spoken blessing: *"O Father, would You bless my son with wisdom and understanding, and with kindness and compassion? Would You cause him to know Your love and Your peace and Your joy, in the name of Jesus?"*

There was no mockery or sarcastic comeback. The son only mumbled a response.

At appropriate times, she continued to bless him—and each of her other children as well. Within a few weeks, her son's entire attitude changed—as did the atmosphere in her home.

These remarkable changes in attitude and peace of mind simply fulfilled the words of the verbal blessing. Do spoken blessings really make that much difference? And if they do...*why* are they so powerful?

That's what this book is about.

Make the Decision

What expectations do you have for this book? What exactly do you want God to do for you as you read it? Most likely you're eager for Him to help you become someone whose life regularly brings words of blessing to others.

If that's true, decide right now to express it in a sincere prayer to the Lord. Ask Him to put His Holy Spirit fully in charge of this learning experience for you and to bring about exactly what He wants to accomplish in your life through this book.

Chapter 2

THE POWER
OF A NAME

"You'll never amount to anything!"

The words rang in Ralph's ears and echoed in his soul. His father had assaulted him with that charge again and again over the years. Nothing Ralph did from the time he was a little boy ever seemed good enough for this stern, perfectionistic father. No matter how hard he tried, he could never earn his dad's unqualified approval.

As he grew up, Ralph closed off his spirit to his father. It was his way of saying, "I'll make you sorry for hurting me, and I'm going to cut you off so you can't hurt me anymore."

In time, however, this young man learned to bless his dad—though it seemed to bring no change in the older man's life or attitudes.

Much later, a doctor stunned his father with a diagnosis of terminal cancer. Realizing he soon would die, his heart was softened. He broke down in tears and asked his son to forgive him for all the ways he had wronged him. Soon he became a believer in Christ and lived out his last days as a transformed man, enjoying fellowship with his son.

Ralph's story shows that giving a blessing may not produce an instant change in the one who is being blessed. However, it freed Ralph from his bitter attitudes toward his dad and allowed God to deal with his father in His own way and timing. This is what God promised to do: "Bless those who persecute you.... 'Vengeance is Mine, I will repay,' says the Lord."[1]

AN UNEXPECTED BLESSING
FOR NEW PARENTS

A good example of someone who was well prepared to speak blessings to others is the man Simeon, in the Gospel of Luke. Simeon's life was marked not only by an undying hope in the coming Messiah, but also by righteousness and devotion to God.[2] More importantly, he had personal experience of the Holy Spirit's presence and power. Simeon lived in Jerusalem, and one day the Spirit guided his steps into the corridors of the great temple. There he saw a certain couple with a newborn baby, seeking the customary rites for dedicating this firstborn infant to God.

Imagine the parents' surprise when old Simeon walked up to them, aglow with the Spirit's fire and warmth, and took their infant in his arms. Luke tells us that Simeon then "blessed God" with beautiful words of praise for this boy—describing Him as God's salvation, as the light of the nations, and as the glory of Israel.

Yes, the baby was Jesus, and as Joseph and Mary heard Simeon's praise for this child, they "marveled at those things which were spoken of Him."[3] And notice what happened next: Turning to these new parents, "Simeon blessed them."

Here was a man devoted to God, a man filled with the Spirit and walking by the Spirit, a man who centered his life on Jesus (for the Spirit had revealed to him "that he would not see death before he had seen the Lord's Christ"[4]). Out of such spiritual realities, there came rising up from within him a blessing for Mary and Joseph—two people who in this extraordinary and challenging season of their lives must have surely appreciated every blessing they could get!

All those spiritual realities—devotion to God, Spirit-dependence, and Christ-centeredness—should be vibrantly true of you and me as well. And as they more and more become realities for us, we'll experience increasing freedom and willingness to quickly take opportunities to bless others, just as Simeon did.

And who can begin to say what joy, power, and freedom such blessings will bring into your world?

THE OVERFLOWING SOURCE

By focusing on each of the three ways God reveals Himself to us—as Father, Son, and Holy Spirit—we understand better how blessing pours into our own lives with a fullness that overflows to others.

When we sing, "Praise God from whom all blessings flow," our words are exactly true. Scripture again and again points to God the Father as the headwaters of a constant stream of blessing for us. But our knowledge of what *blessing* really means can drastically expand when we realize that being blessed is something our Creator Himself experiences and enjoys, to a measureless degree. Our Father in heaven is "the *blessed* God"[5] and "the *blessed* and only Sovereign,"[6] and He is "*blessed* forever."[7] And it's out of His own blessedness that blessings flow our way.

In promising the greatest demonstration of that flow, God equates His blessing of the Holy Spirit poured out on His thirsty people with showers on desert ground: "For I will pour water on the thirsty land, and streams on the dry ground; I will pour my *Spirit* upon your offspring, and my *blessing* on your descendants."[8] Just as is true for God the Father, the blessed Holy Spirit is fully and intricately involved in the blessings we receive.

Master of Blessing

But it's especially in Jesus Christ, the Son of God, that we as human beings learn and experience the most about blessing. Jesus—"who went about doing good"[9]—brought blessing on earth in everything He did and said. He was verbally blessing others right up to His last minute on earth, as He met with His disciples on the Mount of Olives before His ascension: "And lifting up his hands he blessed them. While he blessed them, he parted from them and was carried up into heaven."[10]

Many centuries before this, the psalmist had called out to Christ in praise of the Messiah's blessedness: "Grace is poured upon Your lips; therefore God has blessed You forever."[11] The psalmist foresaw that Christ would speak words of blessing through lips of grace, and those blessings would flow from His own consciousness of being blessed forever by God.

This passage not only exalts Jesus in a unique way, but also points to the seamless connection between the concepts of grace and blessing. We're told early in John's Gospel that Jesus is "full of grace and truth,"[12] and we could just as easily say He's full of *blessing* and truth. A few verses later we read that "from his fullness we have all received, grace upon grace,"[13] or "one blessing after another," as another version translates it. The amazing grace we have in Christ also means amazing blessing. And as He launched into His ministry on earth, both His words and His actions were a stream of blessing like nothing ever seen or heard. In the opening phrases of the Sermon on the Mount, for example, Jesus talked about blessing in a way that exploded its meaning into new dimensions for the people of that day—and this.

There was no doubt about it: *Blessing* was very much on Jesus' mind. He's the Master of blessing. And still is!

In everything He does for us moment by moment, both as our heavenly High Priest interceding for us and as the One indwelling us to accomplish His work in our lives, Jesus continues to bring blessings our way. Every day and every hour for us, in each situation and relationship, what Paul says about Jesus at the beginning of Ephesians always applies: Our loving Father "has blessed us with *every spiritual blessing* in the heavenly places *in Christ.*"[14] It's because we are so blessed ourselves that we can bless others.

Think of it! We can not only experience that life-lifting, joy-charged encouragement from heaven; we can actually *direct* that powerful flow into the hearts of others. Like the worker at the controls of a canal, we can open the floodgates and let the strong river of God's grace surge through us as we bless people in His mighty name.

THE POWER OF THE NAME

So we see that the power of our spoken blessings flows first of all from the abundance of our Creator's own blessedness—and from His wise and loving intention to bless His children with whatever is truly our highest good. When we verbalize a blessing upon others, we have the privilege of taking part in channeling God's goodness to them and in directing them into the Lord's will.

That's why our strongest blessings for others will come when we invoke the mighty name of God, for that name designates His personality, His character, His will, and His heart for blessing all creation. The most powerful blessings begin, then, by simply speaking His name: "The Lord bless you…"

When we center our lives on Christ and allow His Spirit to control us, we find ourselves wanting to do all we can for those we love most—to give them the highest and best gifts we can. And nothing is higher and better than God's blessing. What amazing grace it is that God allows us to be His instruments for directing His blessing into their lives!

MAKE THE DECISION

God really has prepared you to be a channel of spoken blessing to others, hasn't He? Think of how He has abundantly poured out His grace in your life.

No matter how tired you feel or how busy you are, make the decision to spend concentrated time—at the first available moment today or tonight—in thanksgiving and praise to God for His rich supply of blessings in your life. Be as specific as you can in what you thank Him for. Delight His heart as you give Him your gratitude.

And with genuine praise, speak to Him about what His *name* really means *to you*—in terms of His personality, His character, His will, and His heart of blessing.

Chapter 3

THE OVERLOOKED POWER OF OUR WORDS

One day in 1874, at a Gypsy encampment in a place called Epping Forest in England, a carriage drove up with two Americans inside. The two men were accustomed to being surrounded by large crowds in nearby London, for they were none other than the famous evangelist Dwight L. Moody and his musical partner, Ira Sankey. By the prevailing social conventions of the time, however, Gypsies could not expect to be welcomed at the evangelistic meetings the men were holding. Moody and Sankey, therefore, took the gospel out to them.

As the two men stopped and talked to some of the

Gypsies, a group of boys gathered beside the carriage. Ira Sankey reached out and touched the head of one of the youths. "The Lord make a preacher of you, my boy."

The prospects for that coming true, however, seemed dismal at best. The boy, whose mother had died a few years earlier of smallpox, was barely literate and not yet even a Christian, though his father had recently found faith in Christ.

Fifteen years later, Ira Sankey was living in Brooklyn when a rising young British evangelist landed in New York on his first visit to America. He was soon introduced to Sankey, who took him on a carriage drive.

As they passed through Brooklyn's Prospect Park, the evangelist asked Sankey about the meetings with Moody in London years before, and whether he recalled driving out to a Gypsy camp. Sankey replied that he did.

"Do you remember that some little Gypsy boys stood by the wheel," the evangelist continued, "and that, leaning over, you put your hand on the head of one of them and said, 'The Lord make a preacher of you, my boy'?"

"Yes, I remember that, too."

"I am that boy."

Sankey's joy overflowed! And the British evangelist— soon to be well known around the world as "Gypsy" Smith—continued in a ministry that lasted nearly seventy years, influencing millions of lives. For Gypsy Smith, the words Sankey spoke from the carriage that day became an enduring statement of blessing.

"Here I Am..."

It was true in the 1800s and is still true today: Our words have incredible power.

Not long ago a youth pastor stood before the congregation on a Sunday morning and related this account: "When I was a teenager, I used to sit in the back of this auditorium without much interest in God or the Bible. One day the assistant pastor took me aside and said that God had impressed upon him to pray for me. He also believed God was calling me to be a youth pastor!

"At that time, I had no thought or interest in becoming a youth pastor. I had other plans. But his words remained with me, and God changed my heart. I went to Bible school, and now—here I am."

Why do I feel so passionate about the power of words—the power of spoken blessings? Because I have my own story to tell.

When I was about ten years old, I was rowing on a lake one day with a neighbor boy. He wasn't a believer, and there in the boat I began telling him how to become a Christian. He didn't seem at all interested. My effort seemed futile.

A few days later, however, my father told me, "Billy,

I hear that you witnessed to your friend at the lake." I wondered how he knew, since I hadn't mentioned it to anyone. Apparently the boy informed his mother, who must have told my parents.

"Yes," I answered my father.

Then he said, "You are a real little soul-winner!"

I knew that my father's greatest love was leading people to Christ, so his description honored me from my head down to my shoes. I also knew I was unworthy of it, since I didn't actually lead the boy to salvation. I remember clearly thinking, *I'm not worthy of this title, but if I keep growing in the Lord, maybe one day I will be.*

My father's words that day represented such a decisive moment for me that I vividly recall the details of when he uttered them. (We were in our green Chrysler, going west on Hillgrove Avenue, with only the two of us in the car. I was in the backseat, and I can still see the slight turn of his head as he spoke over his shoulder to me.) Empowered by his statement, I began looking for opportunities to bring my friends to gospel meetings. Later, in high school, I made it my goal to explain the gospel to every student. After graduation I began door-to-door witnessing in a small town, and then God used me to lead young Chicago gang members to Christ. I can trace everything that has flowed from my ministry through the years back to that simple word of blessing from my father.

LIFE AND DEATH POWER

The book of Proverbs lays strong emphasis on the power of our words. We're told, for example, how a good word brings gladness to a heart filled with anxiety and depression,[15] and how pleasant words induce sweetness of soul as well as physical health.[16] And listen to this striking statement: *"Death and life are in the power of the tongue."*[17] Our words have lasting impact not only for harm, but also for great good.

I know of a family whose oldest daughter became rebellious in her teen years and eventually ran away from home. As she recounted later, her memory of those years centered on all the fights with her parents and on her father's warning that she would become "just like" the wrong friends she was being drawn to. She admits that a determination to live out his words was part of the reason for her rebellion.

Her younger sister, meanwhile, purposed to remain faithful to the Lord, even if it meant being rejected by her sister. "Ever since I was four or five years old," she relates, "my parents would say to me, 'Lisa, you're going to be our family missionary. God is going to do great things through you in other countries.'" The words pierced her young heart, and those repeated blessings became woven through her strongest childhood memories.

When these parents finally realized this stark difference

in their children's memories, they began to consciously bless their oldest daughter as well. As they did, her life began to change, too. Today she and her husband are growing in the Lord and serving Him, just as the younger daughter is.

WHO WE REALLY ARE

God created the tongue, and He vividly warns us of its destructive power:

> The tongue is a fire, a world of iniquity.… It is an unruly evil, full of deadly poison. With it we bless our God and Father, and with it we curse men, who have been made in the similitude of God. Out of the same mouth proceed blessing and cursing.[18]

Why does the tongue have such devastating power? Because it speaks the thoughts and feelings of the heart, and our hearts are naturally proud and willing to strike out at others. "An evil man out of the evil treasure of his heart brings forth evil. For out of the abundance of the heart his mouth speaks."[19]

Like it or not, our words represent who we really are. They're the living expression of a person's heart, in the same way that Jesus Christ is the living expression of God the Father and is called "the Word."[20] So if Christ, the Master of blessing, dwells within us, and His Spirit directs our thoughts and feelings, our hearts will overflow with the Lord's desire and purpose to bless, spoken in our very own words.

For that reason, although our words have such huge potential for harm, they have even greater potential for good. Light is stronger than darkness! And good overpowers evil—because the sovereign God, the source of all blessing and all good, is infinitely more powerful than anything in creation. A verbal blessing can overrule the effect of any verbal curse.

ONE DAUGHTER'S ANGER

A daughter in a certain family had a reputation for anger. One day her mother stopped her, questioning her conduct in a certain situation. The truth was, she hadn't been angry at all in this particular instance. But then her father pushed his way into the conversation, telling his daughter that she "was an angry person." And that *did* make her angry!

"When he said that," she recalled, "I got very angry and bitter at him and stomped off." She remembers her sister talking with her—trying everything she could think of to help. "But none of it was working. I was just overwhelmed and engulfed in bitterness. I wanted to be free, but I couldn't get freedom…

"After we finally went to bed, I was still crying, and I still felt so hurt. All I could do was lie in bed and sob. The room was just filled with bitterness and hurt. My sister could feel it. Then she remembered about blessing those who curse you, so she said I should do that.

"I had thought about it, but I wouldn't do it. I didn't *want* to! But when she told me to, I decided I would.

"So as I lay in my bed, I sobbed out a blessing for my father. Immediately I was free. The whole room changed—my heart was free.… It worked for me! And then my sister blessed me, and I blessed her, and we have been doing it ever since."

We live in a noisy world, filled with the sounds of verbal putdowns, insults, disrespectful trash talk, and even deliberate curses. God hears all of these offensive things and is grieved by them. His heart longs to hear the sound of His people—children of the light—imparting life-giving blessing to those around them.

There is no mistaking God's standards for the words coming out of our mouths. Paul was about as pointed as he could be when he wrote: "Let no corrupting talk come out of your mouths, but only such as is good for building up, as fits the occasion, that it may give grace to those who hear."[21] For speech that builds others up and gives them grace, as well as offering protection from corrupting influences, nothing surpasses a spoken blessing.

MAKE THE DECISION

Have you understood the power of your words in the lives of others?

Perhaps God has brought to mind someone whose spirit you've wounded by the wrong words. If so, be prompt in confessing this to God (and to the wounded person as well).

Acknowledge before God your true desire for your words to bring enablement, comfort, and encouragement into the lives of others. Agree with Him to let His standard of speech (Ephesians 4:29) become yours as well. Admit to Him that this is impossible in your own strength, and ask Him to teach you how to rely on His Spirit to make this change in your patterns of speaking. And in faith thank Him for how He'll do this!

Chapter 4

THE POWER OF
GOD'S WORDS

What makes a blessing a blessing?

First of all, as we've seen, it involves a vital connection with our blessed God and with His design for blessing all creation. That's why a blessing *in God's name* has such great effect.

We've also seen how it incorporates the simple strength of our own words to greatly influence the lives of others.

And as we'll discover in this chapter, the power of a spoken blessing is amplified also *by invoking God's own words from Scripture*. The strongest verbal blessing, then, includes three powerful forces: God's name, our words, and God's words.

WHAT GOD WANTS TO DO

The Bible allows us to grasp what God wants to accomplish in and through the lives of others. As we catch a glimpse of His desires, we can begin to affirm these things in our blessings.

An Arkansas woman in a troubled marriage—with a history of adultery, numerous separations, and "much anger and hurt and hate"—reported significant changes in their relationship when she learned to bless her husband:

"When I desire to see a quality in his life, I pray it as a blessing for him. So often my thoughts toward my husband have been 'curses,' especially at night before I would go to sleep, replaying the day's hurts and wounds. Now, the last thing I think about at night are blessings for him.

"After about a month of praying blessings for my husband, I am beginning to see a difference in our marriage. His anger has greatly decreased, and we are getting along much better. There has been much less strife and arguing between us. I am enjoying his company more, and I sense that he is enjoying mine more. We are being kind, helpful, and considerate to each other.

"I have hope for my marriage that I never had before, because God's divine power is invoked every day. I look forward to the day when my husband blesses me."

In incorporating specific character qualities into our blessings, as this woman did for her husband, we don't have to rely on our own wish list of how we'd like to see that person change. Instead, we can actually find the character qualities God commands and teaches in the pages of Scripture, relying on the Holy Spirit to impress them on our hearts.

In this way the Lord will give us grace to begin seeing others as He views them, just as Paul teaches us: "From now on, we regard no one according to the flesh,"[22] or "by what the world thinks"[23] or from a "[purely] human point of view."[24] In our new life in Christ, we're freed from that kind of narrow outlook on others and *can* increasingly see their strengths, gifts, weaknesses, and needs—all from God's perspective.

God has eternal purposes for every person in the world. He wants each one to discover those purposes and fulfill them. This is the basis of true success. God's words, meanwhile, are living and eternal messages to us through His Spirit and address every need a person could ever have. When we bless others, we can speak forth the biblical goals and biblical answers God has for them. In this way, we begin to impart to them the desire and power to truly *live those words out*—empowered by the active work of Christ in their lives and the strong help of the indwelling Holy Spirit.

UNDERSTANDING NEEDS

As you consider your loved ones and how to better understand what to pray for them and how to bless them, ask God for wisdom and understanding. He delights to grant us insights and discernment through the pages of His Word and the still, small voice of the Counselor, the Holy Spirit.

But this is no casual exercise! Finding the most appropriate biblical promises and commands to speak in blessing to others requires both time and effort. As you keep your mind open to His direction, you might begin to ask yourself questions like these:

- Do they love the Lord with all their heart, soul, mind, and strength?
- Are they regularly enjoying personal time with Him in prayer and His Word?
- Are they depending fully on Jesus Christ their Savior and the indwelling power of His Spirit for their acceptance in God's eyes, rather than trying to please Him and live for Him in their own power?
- Are they experiencing consistent joy and peace through fully trusting the Lord in all kinds of circumstances and trials?
- Are they consciously depending on the Spirit's giftedness and serving others in love?

- Are they actively walking in the Spirit's power as a witness to unbelievers they're around?
- Are they regularly leaning on God's guidance in their lives so they can walk in the good works He has prepared for them?[25]
- Are they submitting to God-ordained authorities and to His discipline in their lives?
- Is anything in their lives competing with their walk with the Lord?
- What temptations seem to have the strongest attraction to them?
- What fears or hurts or pressures are they dealing with?

All these needs can be addressed in private prayer for others as well as in a verbal blessing. As you speak the blessing, the Lord will use His mighty name and His living Word to work in the lives of your loved ones.

Count on it. He will!

A FRAMEWORK TO BUILD UPON

Once you see words, phrases, and concepts in Scripture that you believe God wants you to pray and claim for someone else, how do you bring them together in the form of a blessing?

The truth is, God has already given us the perfect

framework in His Word. At the end of the sixth chapter in the Old Testament book of Numbers, we find one of the most beautiful and appealing portions in all of Scripture. It's a blessing God entrusted into the hands of Israel's priesthood in order to bless the people.

And since by the blood of Christ all believers have been made into "a holy priesthood, to offer up spiritual sacrifices acceptable to God through Jesus Christ,"[26] this priestly blessing in Numbers 6 is now fully our own to use in blessing others. Listen to this passage:

> "The LORD bless you and keep you;
> the LORD make His face shine upon you,
>   and be gracious to you;
> the LORD lift up His countenance upon you,
>   and give you peace."[27]

We'll study these verses more closely in the next chapter. For now, recognize that by using this priestly blessing as a framework, we can add other scriptural words and concepts. In doing so, we invoke God's power to actually fulfill these Scriptures in another person's life.

PUTTING IT ALL TOGETHER

Let's imagine a young person you know struggles with fear and anxiety. You ask God to guide you to the right passages to pray for this person and then use a concordance to look up *fear* and *anxious*. The concordance directs you to verses like these:

- "For God has not given us a spirit of fear, but of power and of love and of a sound mind."[28]
- "There is no fear in love; but perfect love casts out fear, because fear involves torment. But he who fears has not been made perfect in love."[29]
- "Be anxious for nothing, but in everything by prayer and supplication, with thanksgiving, let your requests be made known to God; and the peace of God, which surpasses all understanding, will guard your hearts and minds through Christ Jesus."[30]

You can then take the basic ideas in the verses and put them into the framework of the biblical blessing in Numbers 6, as a blessing to speak upon your young friend. The result could be something like this.

"May the Lord God bless you and keep you from the torment of fear and anxiety. May He cause His face to shine upon you with power, love, and a sound mind and give you grace to cast out fear through perfect love. May He lift up His countenance upon you with freedom as you tell Him every detail of your need in earnest, thankful prayer, and give you the peace that surpasses all understanding as He keeps your heart and mind safe through Jesus Christ."

MORE EXAMPLES OF
WORD-CENTERED BLESSINGS

Early in 2 Corinthians, Paul speaks these words of praise: "Blessed be the God and Father of our Lord Jesus Christ, the Father of mercies and God of all comfort."[31] For someone enduring deep sorrow, those words and thoughts—in combination with expressions from Numbers 6—might be adapted into a verbal blessing like this:

"May the God and Father of our Lord Jesus Christ, the God of all comfort, comfort your heart and protect you from discouragement. May He cause His face to shine upon you as you rejoice in troubles and trials, and give you grace to respond with His love and good works. May the Lord lift up His countenance upon you with the riches of His joy and pleasure, and give you His peace in your heart and soul."

The apostle Peter includes a blessing near the close of his first letter: "May the God of all grace, who called us to His eternal glory by Christ Jesus, after you have suffered a while, perfect, establish, strengthen, and settle you."[32] How, then, could we use this passage in a blessing—perhaps to strengthen the heart of someone enduring a severe trial? Perhaps we could put together wording similar to the following:

"May the God of all grace, who has called you to His eternal glory by Christ Jesus, bless you and keep you strong during this time of testing. May He cause His face to shine upon you

and give you grace to endure suffering for His sake. May He lift up His countenance upon you to make you perfect, and after your sufferings are over, may He establish, strengthen, and settle you with His peace."

In his letter to the Romans, Paul writes these words of blessing to promote unity among believers:

> Now may the God of patience and comfort grant you to be like-minded toward one another, according to Christ Jesus, that you may with one mind and one mouth glorify the God and Father of our Lord Jesus Christ. Therefore receive one another, just as Christ also received us, to the glory of God.[33]

This marvelous passage could be turned into a blessing for anyone who may struggle in relationships with other Christians:

"May the God of patience and comfort bless you by keeping you like-minded with other believers. May He cause His face to shine upon you so you can walk in the fellowship of His light and so that with other believers you may with one mind and one mouth glorify God. May the Lord give you grace to receive others as Christ also received you. May the Father of our Lord Jesus Christ lift up His countenance upon you and give you the peace and oneness of spirit that will glorify God and cause the world to believe that He sent His Son into the world."

What an encouragement! Can you imagine someone placing a hand on your shoulder and praying those words for you? And please remember…these are more than merely beautiful words, for they invoke the power and grace and blessing of almighty God.

For an endless variety of situations and circumstances, the Lord will lead us to all kinds of words and phrases in the Bible that can be easily adapted as blessings. For example, for those who work full time in ministry, Paul sets a noble pattern in this promise he made to the Roman believers: "I know that when I come to you I will come in the fullness of the blessing of Christ."[34] What a worthy aim and standard to use today as a blessing in sending out Christian workers in Christ's power and encouragement to their work in the harvest fields of the kingdom.

Many other passages provide this same kind of help for us in developing verbal blessings. (At the end of this book you'll find a helpful list of prayer passages in the Scriptures that especially lend themselves to adaptation into a blessing upon others.) The more we study and apply the truths of Scripture, the more effective we will be in expressing verbal blessings.

Make the Decision

Are you getting the picture of just how dynamic spoken blessings can be?

In the next chapter, we'll be diving into a careful study of the amazing blessing in Numbers 6. This will require your close attention and reflection. Decide now to give this foundational passage your full concentration, and ask God to help you understand this model blessing in a life-changing way.

Meanwhile, in this chapter you just finished, look at the long list of questions under the heading "Understanding Needs." Think of someone whose life you want to bless. With that person in mind, go through that list of questions and begin thinking about the kind of blessing you want to speak into his or her life. (Make a mental note to return to this list of questions as needed, to help guide your thinking in being more sensitive to how you can bless others.)

This could be a good time also to explore a few of the passages in the list of "Bible Passages for Words of Blessing" at the end of this book. You may find yourself drawn to some of these more than others. Let them become your friends for life, as you carry over their powerful words into your own spoken blessings for others.

Chapter 5

OUR MODEL
BLESSING

There's nothing more valuable to any human being than being blessed by our Creator and Savior. His blessing means a profound experience of His grace, His goodness, and even His approval. Anything truly good we could ever desire in life—for ourselves as well as for those we love—comes wrapped in the blessings our Lord loves to bestow.

What an astonishing thought it is, then, that God is eager for you and me to have a part in bringing down those blessings to the people around us. That's why He takes the initiative, early in Scripture, to show His people how to do just that.

A CLEAR AND BEAUTIFUL PATTERN
"This is the way you shall bless the children of Israel...."

That's the plain and simple introduction to the potent words of blessing we find at the end of Numbers 6. God gave these clear instructions to Aaron and the priests at the same point in history that He first established their priesthood (as the people of Israel prepared to leave Sinai and cross the wilderness toward the Promised Land). In His overflowing grace, God was so set on blessing His people that He gave their worship leaders the very words they needed to regularly speak His blessing upon the people.

God also gives these words to you and me. In freeing us from our sins by His blood, Jesus has made us to be "priests to His God and Father";[35] we're "a royal priesthood" because we're His holy and chosen people.[36] The priestly privilege of blessing others, then, is ours to make the most of, and these words in Numbers 6 are our model and ideal.

Does this mean those words are a "formula" we must follow whenever we want to bless someone? No, an effective spoken blessing may take an endless variety of expression. But these Spirit-inspired words in Numbers 6 truly capture the essence of what a blessing is all about. They're a priceless gift from our loving Lord, a treasure we don't want to neglect.

This blessing in reality is a triple blessing; it has a simple three-part structure, each part beginning with the

Lord's name. Ever since the church began, God's people have viewed each of these three parts as corresponding to one of the members of the Trinity—first the Father (as our protector), then the Son (as our means of grace), and finally the Holy Spirit (as the sustainer of our peace.)

Each of the three parts in turn has two concise phrases. The wording is dignified and formal—yet shines out with great warmth and light.

I urge you to memorize this brief and beautiful passage phrase by phrase, which I think you'll find surprisingly easy to do. Keep this incomparable blessing ready in your heart to flow freely through your lips to accomplish great things in the lives of others around you.

Let's look more closely now at each of the six parts in this blessing.

"THE LORD BLESS YOU..."

The Lord, of course, is the source of all blessing. He is the mighty headwaters of blessing, and we are merely His channels for directing it into the lives of others. That's why the most compelling spoken blessings will begin by acknowledging His name.

God's blessing represents His goodness in action—like a steady, gentle rain falling on once-barren ground. Receiving this flow of blessing is what we were created for. In Genesis 1, as we read how God created man in His own image, male and female, we immediately find these words: "Then God blessed them."[37] It's His blessing alone that makes our lives what they were meant to be, and we can't be satisfied until we have it.

All around us are so many people who cry out to God from the depths of their heart, praying as Jabez prayed: "Oh, that You would bless me indeed!"[38] They long for relief from spiritual dryness and emptiness, and nothing except God's own hand of blessing can quench that thirst.

"AND KEEP YOU..."

When Jabez cried out for the Lord's blessing, he also specifically asked God to keep him from harm or from evil.[39] The Lord "keeps" us by guarding and protecting us from sin and from our enemy the devil, just as Jesus prayed for His followers: "I do not pray that You should take them out of the world, but that You should keep them from the evil one."[40] God Himself is the One "who is able to keep you from stumbling."[41]

The word *keep* is such a warm, comforting word. We keep things that we treasure. We tuck them away, safe from harm, because they're valuable and precious to us. The Hebrew word used here speaks of guarding, protecting, and encompassing about with a hedge for safety.

What a moving thought that the Lord would desire to

keep us in His care, as His unique and special treasures.
And what a privilege it is to call such a blessing down on
someone else.

The Lord's protective "keeping" of us is often a task
that God's angels accomplish: "For He shall give His angels
charge over you, to keep you in all your ways."[42]

Do you know believers who are often exposed to
spiritual temptation and opposition because of their work
or ministry? Such persons in particular can be encouraged
and strengthened as you offer the spoken blessing of God's
protective keeping.

"THE LORD MAKE HIS FACE SHINE UPON YOU..."

The second part of the priestly blessing is meant to bring
others into a conscious awareness of God's smile upon their
lives, a smile that dispels darkness and pierces the deepest
gloom. It floods our soul like sunshine in a room where a
long-shuttered window is finally opened.

Just as growing things need the light of the sun for their
very survival, so spiritual life cannot grow or blossom without the brightness that comes from the face of the One who
is light Himself.[43]

Because of Christ's indwelling presence, the blazing
radiance of the Lord's face penetrates our deepest being, just

as Paul explains: "For God, who said, 'Let light shine out of darkness,' has shone in our hearts to give the light of the knowledge of the glory of God in the face of Jesus Christ."[44] No wonder Jesus our Savior is called "the Sun of Righteousness"[45] and "the true Light which gives light to every man."[46] His light is a welcome warmth, reaching into every shadowy corner and crevice of our lives. This light never glows brighter in our lives than when we're genuinely trusting God amid our own trials and tribulations. It's like a lighthouse's beam shining out of a dark and stormy sky. Others who know of our trials can see our radiant face and hope as we endure them, and they're blessed to realize how God Himself can be the only explanation for this.

"AND BE GRACIOUS TO YOU..."

The sunlight of the Lord's face opens the way for His grace to pour into our lives. As we saw earlier, the reality of blessing and blessedness is closely interwoven with the biblical concept of grace. Blessing flows from grace, and blessedness is always the result of grace.

It's through God's grace in Christ that we not only experience salvation but also the desire and the power to carry out God's will. It's His grace that also brings us spiritual giftedness, the gifts that are meant to be a source of help and hope to others if we don't neglect or misuse them.

In the New Testament, we're taught that our speech

should "impart grace to the hearers."[47] To verbally bestow the blessing of God's grace is a strong and effective way to do exactly that.

Do you know believers whose lives seem clouded by striving and the bearing of burdens too heavy for them to carry? Bless them with the blessing of the Lord's light and grace, as He Himself carries those burdens for us and leaves us with His shining joy in their place.

"THE LORD LIFT UP HIS COUNTENANCE UPON YOU..."

The final part of the priestly blessing includes a biblical expression that means giving one's full visual and mental attention to someone in a favorable way. To "lift up one's countenance" toward someone is to turn in that person's direction and establish eye contact. It implies a nearness and a connection of spirit.

You've most likely experienced that with a close friend—or maybe your spouse. You have something on your heart you want to share, and when you glance up at your friend, you find him or her fully engaged in what you're saying. Looking into that person's eyes, you see interest, warmth, and concern—rather than boredom, impatience, or distraction. What a gift it is to have someone's full and compassionate attention! How blessed we are if we have friends who truly *listen* to us.

That is what you and I experience as God lifts up His countenance upon us. The indwelling of God's Holy Spirit is His most intense and intimate way of establishing and maintaining this constant connection with His children on earth. In the Spirit we have the Lord's never-faltering focus toward us, as He teaches, guides, and encourages us.

"AND GIVE YOU PEACE"

Peace is the final aspect of the priestly blessing. The Hebrew term in this verse is *shalom,* a word that embraces so much more than our English word *peace*. *Shalom* includes wholeness, health, security, serenity, well-being, and contentment, plus friendship and harmony with God and with other people. It means an absence of negative stress, disturbance, tension, or conflict. The ultimate blessing for our daily lives is to experience such comprehensive peace with God, with other people, and with ourselves.

In the New Testament, Paul tells us that the kingdom of God is "righteousness and peace and joy in the Holy Spirit."[48] Experiencing this peace means aiming for a life that is Spirit-centered instead of worldly-centered, for "to set the mind on the flesh is death, but to set the mind on the Spirit is life and *peace*."[49]

This peace is intimately associated not only with the Holy Spirit but also with Jesus Christ, the Prince of Peace. "For He Himself is our peace."[50] It's a peace that comes our way at great cost to Himself, for His task on earth was "making peace by the blood of his cross."[51]

Remember our Savior's wonderful promise? "Peace I leave with you, My peace I give to you; not as the world gives do I give to you. Let not your heart be troubled, neither let it be afraid."[52] It's "the peace of God, which surpasses all understanding"[53]—something utterly different from any kind of security or serenity the world can possibly offer.

Do you know those who are restless and troubled? Do you have loved ones who can't seem to escape inner turmoil? Bless them with the blessing of peace.

GOD'S NAME UPON US

After imparting these beautiful lines of blessing to the Old Testament priests, the Lord concluded with these words: "So they shall put My name on the children of Israel, and I will bless them."[54] *To bless the people with these weighty words was actually a way to place the Lord's name upon them.* Think of it! Through the act of blessing people you know with these words, you are linking them with the beauty, peace, and power of God's own name…the name that has existed since before Creation, before time, and will last forever and ever.

In striking images and expressions, the Psalms tell us that God's name is the source of our salvation, our help, and our victory[55] so that we can boldly proclaim, "His name alone is exalted."[56] We accurately praise Him when we say, "O LORD, our Lord, how excellent is Your name in all the earth!"[57]

God, whose name is "I AM WHO I AM"[58]—this God actually places that holy and exalted name upon His people as we verbally bless them. What an incredible truth! What stronger way can there be for Him to show that we belong to Him as His treasured and cherished possessions?

It reminds us today of John's heavenly vision in which he saw the name of the Lamb and the name of God the Father written on the foreheads of those who follow Jesus.[59] The Lord's name is our greatest honor and pride as well as our protection.

As we remember how "the name of the LORD is a strong tower" where the righteous find refuge,[60] we'll be eager to offer a blessing in the Lord's name to all those who need His security, nurture, and enablement. As you continue to reflect on each part of this richly worded passage in Numbers 6, ask God to make you sensitive to those around you whom He wants you to bless with these words. Ask Him to open your spiritual eyes and ears to what He wants to accomplish in their lives. Offer God's own blessing upon them, and with confident faith expect Him to accomplish these things in His own perfect timing.

As our Lord said so clearly, "Freely you have received, freely give."[61]

MAKE THE DECISION

Are you beginning to see why so many people have found the blessing in Numbers 6:24–26 to be such an incredibly rich and beautiful passage?

Make the decision to memorize these verses immediately and to have them written on your heart for the rest of your life as a guiding framework for speaking blessing to others.

Who has God brought to mind as you've explored this priestly blessing? Is there someone you know who needs protection because of frequent exposure to spiritual opposition? Do you know of someone feeling burdened who needs to know God's smile and His grace? Is there someone restless and troubled who needs the Lord's peace? Pray for them now. And be ready to speak blessing into their lives when you can. (You may find it especially helpful to write down the word of blessing ahead of time. This is excellent practice!)

Consider also taking a moment now to explore a few more of the passages in the list of "Bible Passages for Words of Blessing" at the end of this book. Make it your goal to look up every passage on that list in order to become more familiar with biblical patterns of prayer and blessing.

Chapter 6

BLESSING OUR CHILDREN

The home is the arena where giving blessings will most often touch our hearts and lives with the greatest repercussion.

In a family in Maryland with three daughters, the oldest describes the immediate impact of receiving their father's blessing: "He sits us in a circle and puts his hands on ours and prays a blessing individually on each of my sisters, my mother, and me. He asks God to give me strength and wisdom because I am a leader; he prays that I will lead my younger siblings in the right direction, along with the children and teenagers in our church.

"He then prays a blessing on my sister, who is fourteen—that she won't follow the wrong crowd and that she would always have a sweet spirit.

"He prays that my eleven-year-old sister will follow the right crowd and that she will have a servant's spirit, willing to help out in any area of the home and the church.

"Every time my father gets through blessing us, the most amazing thing happens. My sisters and I don't quarrel! My eleven-year-old sister will hug me and tell me that she loves me. I do the same to her. Before being blessed, we would never do that!… My sisters and I are getting closer and closer, and our family devotions have more meaning."

Parents who walk consistently with the Lord and verbally bless their children from a sincere spirit of love often see an immediate impact.

Scripture makes it clear, however, that blessing our children isn't some magic formula to guarantee their spiritual or physical well-being. David blessed his son Absalom on one occasion—but the words fell on hard, stony ground, and there was no response.[62] The young man turned on his own brother in a murderous, vengeful way—and then on his father as well. It's always true that the children we bless are fully free to choose whether they will receive that blessing and live wisely according to it, or disregard it and turn their backs on God.

Nevertheless, to leave our children a heritage of many

spoken blessings is one of the wisest and most loving things we can do for them.

A LONG TIME COMING

For some, the joy of a father's blessing can be long in coming.

One young woman whose childhood memories were mostly negative heard a message about gratefulness at one of our ministry's seminars. She knew God especially wanted her to apply it in her relationship with her father.

"I started with the only thing I could come up with— 'Thank You, Lord, that I have my father's green eyes.' Doesn't sound like much, does it? But it was the beginning of a change that led to a very dear relationship with my dad and big changes in me.

"Over the years, God brought to my remembrance more and more things for which I could be thankful. Before I knew it, I was writing those things down and sending them to my father in letters.

"When I was twenty-nine, I moved home to help Dad take care of Mother during her last three months of life. During that time, I must have flared up at him about something, because I remember going to him one night, kneeling beside his bed, and in tears asking him to forgive me for my attitude. It was a major turning point in our relationship.

"I continued to send letters of thanks to my dad, and I watched as our relationship slowly changed…

"Then I married, and my stepmother thought my father would have a heart attack trying to walk me down the aisle. He was so proud!

"After I had been married for several years, my husband and I were sitting with my father on our porch. My husband lovingly asked my father why he was so sarcastic. (I wanted to kick my husband and quiet him, but God had other plans.)

"My father explained something I hadn't realized. He never knew what it was like to be told, 'I love you.' (In fact I remember, as a little girl, going to my grandma and granddad's house and watching Daddy put his arm around his mom to hug her. She never responded except to verbally say, 'Hi, Oliver,' and to keep the table full of food.)

"Dad flunked out of high school, then went to summer school and graduated. Then he did poorly in college, so he left to join the marines. Later he went back to college on the GI Bill, making straight A's the first year, with some B's afterwards. He made the Chemistry Society. When he offhandedly mentioned this to his dad, his father responded with, 'Well, I guess you think you're somebody now, don't you?'

"As my father told my husband and me about these things, lights went on all over my heart. It opened up a whole new understanding of Dad.

"One day my husband came home from work to find me sitting on the living room floor, holding a letter from Daddy and crying. Bob asked if it was a good letter or a bad letter. I responded, 'I've waited forty years for this letter!' The letter told me how proud of me he was. It was my father's blessing.

"Right before my father died two years ago, my husband and children allowed me to spend his last months helping my stepmother take care of him. This is a time I will never regret giving to him. I not only helped with his care, but I also shared memories and was able to tell him how much I love him."

MORE LOVE, MORE BLESSING

Should we give a spoken blessing to our children every day? Some parents do, and there are good reasons why we should try to give a blessing regularly. Children who experience spiritual benefit from the blessing look forward to receiving it whenever they can.

One mother reports, "We have noticed several things happen in our family as we apply the lessons we have learned regarding the 'spoken blessing.' We are all demonstrating more love toward each other, attitudes really are transformed, and the children are growing in faith!

"Our children will come to us and report that one of their siblings needs a blessing because he or she has a bad attitude or is being naughty. All of us then gather around and bless the 'offender.' This act demonstrates great love toward him or her. No need for the children to be telling tales or taking matters into their own hands, as they now have a practical solution to the situation.

"Whenever my husband and I notice a wrong attitude in a child, that child receives a blessing, and I am continually amazed how attitudes are changed immediately. Sometimes a little talk is required, but the spoken blessing is the transformer....

"Our children now come to us and ask for a blessing.... I frequently get asked to give a 'school blessing,' particularly for math! A sports blessing is another favorite, or help with 'I can't seem to get myself going' attitudes.

"Our ten-year-old son blesses me several times each day, every day. This is truly exciting!"

GETTING OVER THE AWKWARDNESS

It can often be awkward at first for a parent to speak a blessing upon a child, and it can be awkward as well for the child to receive it. This awkwardness, however, doesn't diminish the blessing's power. And many can testify that the awkwardness in time disappeared, and they now rejoice over the blessing and look forward to it.

There's benefit in faithfully imparting a blessing in the family even when you don't feel like it. A young woman raised in a loving Christian home described how doubts, anger, and bitterness began to fill her mind as she grew older. She allowed a wall of hurt and self-centeredness to build up in her heart, shutting out God as well as her family's deepest love.

During this time, her father read about the power of spoken blessings and decided to implement this in their home. "One day he asked my brother and me if we would be willing to pray and bless each other, the three of us together. First my dad would pray a blessing upon my brother and me. Next we would pray a blessing on him.

"I didn't want to bless my dad. My heart and mind were filled with anger and distrust toward him for allowing certain things into my life. (In reality, those things were really of my own doing.)

"As the three of us were kneeling, my dad looked at me, and with tears streaming down his face he said, 'Why don't you want to bless me? Are you that filled with hate and anger toward me? I've always had only your best interest in mind. I'm still human and make mistakes.'

"By this time he was weeping, and my brother, who is rarely moved to tears, was misty eyed. Both of them began praying and pleading with me to soften my heart and turn back to the heavenly Father. I finally agreed to bless them both.

"I don't remember what I said, but I do know that the

spoken blessing proved to be a powerful tool. It wasn't until a few months later that I truly and finally surrendered my all on the altar and got back on the right track. It wasn't an instant breakthrough for me, but I do know that when I blessed my father with my will—in spite of all my feelings—God began a work of healing in our relationship.

"Those words spoken out of obedience began a great work and miracle of tearing down the strong tower Satan was using to destroy my life. Praise God…God has used this concept of speaking a blessing to change my life."

IN TRAINING AND DISCIPLINE

A spoken blessing has particular value in the process of training children and shaping their development as they grow out of immaturity in the different areas of their lives.

An emotionally disturbed orphan was having a continual problem with bed-wetting. His host family gave him a verbal blessing, asking God to deliver him from his fears and to bless him with self-control, security, and peace. After the first blessing, the bed-wetting stopped.

Another parent reports what happened when their seven-year-old son experienced a problem with sulkiness and gloom that worsened over a period of months. "Every attempt we made to correct the problem failed. We had reached a point of exasperation." Then they learned about the power of the spoken blessing, which revealed to them their son's need for a blessing.

"I gathered the other children around and blessed Samuel. I asked the Lord to bless him with a radiant countenance, joy in his heart, and a beautiful smile that ministered into the life of others. As I was speaking his little face lit up, his chest puffed out, and he just kept smiling. I spoke that same blessing to him once more that same week.

"It has been around six months now, and I am very happy to report that the change in Samuel has been miraculous. He keeps smiling, he has a radiant joy about him, and the first thing we notice about Samuel in the morning is a beautiful, radiant smile and a very enthusiastic 'Good morning!'

"This has truly been a work of the Lord, for all of our own efforts failed.... In simple faith we have been obedient and have witnessed the power of the spoken blessing."

A blessing can be spoken effectively by a parent even while administering discipline to a child. The blessing at this time should emphasize God's love for the child and His great purposes for the child.

By blessing the child during a time of discipline, the parent will be greatly helped in overcoming any anger or frustration and will, instead, have a spirit of patience and love. It helps to remember that the primary goal of discipline is not to bring the child under the parents' authority, but under God's authority.

BLESSING BY FAITH

Scripture tells us that it was "by faith" that Isaac and Jacob blessed their children.[63] Blessing their children was an act of faith. Today, in our own faith, you and I possess what Isaac and Jacob in their lifetimes did not—the joy of the gospel and the knowledge of Christ. How much more then should we gladly bless our children in the power and the riches of our faith in the Lord!

Such gladness can be particularly expressed in a blessing by adding the element of music.

A woman in North Carolina has this recollection: "My father blessed each one of us eight children when we were born. He wrote a song of blessing for us. He would look into our eyes and sing a catchy little tune using the meanings of our names, with an exhortation he wanted to come true for our lives and a related Scripture verse.

"He has continued to sing our special songs to us throughout our lives…. Now that I am older, I can recognize how motivating this blessing has been for me. Also, I recognize that I cannot fulfill this blessing in my own strength, so I have begun praying for the Lord to build those qualities in me."

Songs, indeed, are often very effective in communicating a blessing to another person, especially when parents sing a blessing to their children. Remember how we're instructed in Scripture to speak to one another "in psalms and hymns and spiritual songs, singing and making melody in your heart to the Lord."[64] The bestowing of a blessing is a perfect occasion for living out this command.

When children came to Jesus, "He took them up in His arms, laid His hands on them, and blessed them."[65] Blessing our children is like putting them into Jesus' arms to lift up and to have Him embrace them and bless them Himself.

MAKE THE DECISION

Even if you aren't a parent, you have opportunity to touch children's lives with words of blessing.

Think of at least one child you know, some boy or girl to whom you feel the Lord would like you to speak a blessing. Practice what you might say to this child by writing out a blessing, using the patterns and resources you've learned about in this book.

🍃

Chapter 7

BLESSING OUR ENEMIES

Ten-year-old Elena was sleeping in her bed one night when a scorpion climbed onto her leg and stung her. She screamed with pain, awaking the rest of the family.

Elena's mother understood exactly how her daughter felt. She too had been stung by an Arizona bark scorpion, the most poisonous scorpion species in the American Southwest, where Elena's parents served as missionaries to Native Americans. For Elena's mother, the results were excruciating pain and swelling, followed by weakness, dizziness, tightening of her throat, and a tingling in her limbs that continued for weeks.

Elena suffered none of these effects, however. After her

mother's experience, the family discovered an unusual and effective antidote for just such an emergency—a small battery-powered electrical unit developed by their mission organization that produced a high-voltage, low-current charge. They attached electrodes to their daughter's leg and applied the charge to the area of the sting. The girl's pain stopped immediately, and she experienced only a slight, temporary soreness where the venom had entered.

This kind of electrical antidote has been used with various kinds of poisonous bites, with many positive results. Though doctors aren't fully sure why it works, the charge of the current somehow neutralizes the venom.

Scripture tells us about an even worse venom. The tongue, James writes, is "an unruly evil, full of deadly poison."[66] And when someone is bitten by the poison of another's words, a spoken blessing acts just like the electric charge to neutralize the pain and destruction.

NOT OUR NATURAL REACTION

Of course, when someone verbally abuses us, returning a blessing is seldom if ever our natural reaction. We would much rather strike back with damaging words of our own. Our pride prompts us to return hurt for hurt and insult for insult. This, however, only doubles the venom and the destruction of the original abuse.

Nevertheless, we feel we can't just sit there and take it; we've got to do *something*.

God is aware of that natural tendency on our part, and He makes provision for it. He gives us an appropriate response to make—though it isn't what comes naturally! Instead, He tells us to depend on His grace and His Spirit's enabling, and to answer back with words of blessing. "Bless those who persecute you," Scripture tells us; "bless and do not curse."[67]

This spoken blessing for those who verbally hurt us is part of the larger response Jesus taught us of always loving our enemies. It's a response that combines both words of love and actions of love: "You have heard that it was said, 'You shall love your neighbor and hate your enemy.' But I say to you, love your enemies, bless those who curse you, do good to those who hate you, and pray for those who spitefully use you and persecute you."[68]

If we bless those who abuse or curse us, God will bless us and will also take full responsibility for whatever punishment needs to happen in the lives of our offenders.

> "Beloved, do not avenge yourselves, but rather give place to wrath; for it is written, 'Vengeance is Mine, I will repay,' says the Lord. Therefore 'If your enemy is hungry, feed him; If he is thirsty, give him a drink; For in so doing you will heap

coals of fire on his head.' Do not be overcome by evil, but overcome evil with good."[69]

LASTING HURTS

When Scripture speaks of blessing those who "curse" us, this cursing can include insults, reproaches, and verbal offenses of all kinds that may come our way. Many people struggle for weeks or months or even years with the consequences of such a spoken curse. And it can come from quite unexpected sources.

Before going to college, one young person took a short-term job in a ministry organization in Australia and bore the brunt of insensitive remarks from a supervisor—"telling me that I was stupid or that I had no life skills." Those words couldn't be forgotten. "I carried that hurt to college, and without knowing it I was in bondage to a curse....

"I started struggling in school and failed three exams in a row. I had never had problems with school before. I then became consumed with my studies so I would not fail any more exams. I lost my focus so that God was not number one in my life. I had sacrificed my relationships with people and ultimately my time with the Lord by working on projects and my studies.

"One day when I was on summer break, the Lord really spoke to me. I realized that I could not honestly say that I loved the Lord with all of my heart, soul, mind, and strength."

About the same time, this student heard a message about the value of blessing those who curse us. "I went into my room and closed the door…I cried out to God to bless me, and I asked Him to bless my former supervisor and his family. Instantly I felt as if chains had been lifted off of me. I felt an incredible freedom that I had not experienced before.

"The joy that I now feel is overwhelming…."

Although a "curse" of any kind is always a powerful tool for evil, a blessing is a much more powerful tool for good.

REVILING

One of the terms in Scripture for someone who speaks abusive words is *reviler*. Reviling comes from a heart of scorn and contempt. It's the spewing out of anger and hatred in a verbal attack upon another. Its purpose is to vilify, to defame, to bring shame, to discredit, or to attribute evil and sinister motives to another. It's to rail on a person.

Another aspect of reviling is ridicule. To ridicule is to hold up a person or his ideas to laughter. It's to sneer, scoff, and belittle that person. Ridicule is an expression of disdain. A common method of ridicule is giving someone a label that's associated with something evil, unpopular, or ridiculous.

Reviling is a serious sin in God's sight. Paul tells us not to keep company with any believer who happens to be a reviler,[70] and he adds that revilers are among those who will never inherit God's kingdom.[71]

Jesus Himself was reviled. We remember how the Roman soldiers not only scourged Him but mocked and belittled Him, and while He hung on the cross, He was mocked and scorned by those looking on. "Even the robbers who were crucified with Him reviled Him."[72]

Yet even on the cross, Jesus blessed His persecutors by praying, "Father, forgive them, for they do not know what they do."[73] "When he was reviled, he did not revile in return; when he suffered, he did not threaten, but continued entrusting himself to him who judges justly."[74] In this way Jesus marks out our own right response to attacks from others. "For to this you were called, because Christ also suffered for us, leaving us an example, that you should follow His steps."[75]

The apostle Peter specifically points to our need to bless those who revile us: "Do not repay evil for evil or reviling for reviling, but on the contrary, bless, for to this you were called, that you may obtain a blessing."[76] The apostle Paul followed this pattern: "Being reviled," he said, "we bless."[77]

The immediate rewards of blessing a reviler are freedom from an emotional reaction and genuine love for the one doing the reviling. Most everyone who has been involved in a public ministry of some sort has experienced personal attacks. When I experience the venomous sting of a reviler, it causes deep anguish in the pit of my stomach. If I do nothing about it, this anguish increases in intensity and in emotional grief. But when I ask God, out loud, to bless those who have reviled me, I can honestly say that the hurtful emotions that were there clear up, and in their place I experience a sincere love for the reviler. There's also confidence that God will both bless me and deal with the reviler in ways that will bring glory to Him.

A BLESSING FOR AN ABUSER

Of course the hurt and oppression we experience from others can be much more than verbal abuse. But even then, returning a blessing is the biblical response.

A teenager in Canada explained an eleven-year battle with depression stemming from an incident at age seven of sexual abuse by a babysitter. It was a struggle that couldn't be overcome by psychiatric counseling: "It helped to share my feelings," the teenager wrote, "but as time passed, the memory and pain would come back in a deeper way. There was never any true freedom from the bitterness and guilt that I had toward this girl and myself."

A breakthrough finally came through talking with a godly counselor who looked to the Scriptures: "He shared with me from his life how he had experienced bitterness toward certain people he had worked with and how God brought freedom to his life through blessing his enemies.

"He then shared with me the passage of Matthew 18:23–35, where we find the story of the two servants who owed a debt. He showed me how I was like the servant who had been forgiven a great debt, and I had then turned toward my fellow servant and refused forgiveness of her lesser debt. Through my unforgivingness, I had been delivered to the tormentors of depression and bitterness. He shared with me…that the key to finding freedom could be found in blessing her.

"As I began to think things over, a war was raging within me. I could not bring myself to bless this girl, especially after what she had done to me. But the more I looked at the passage, the more I knew in my heart that I needed to bless her.

"We then knelt in prayer, but my heart was so heavy I wasn't able to speak. This man prayed, asking the Lord to rebuke Satan, his principalities, and his powers over my life. I was then able to speak from my heart.

"As I began to ask the Lord to bless her, the load of guilt I had been carrying started to lift off my shoulders.… Once I finished praying, I was free…

"Over a year later, I have had a few times where the memories of the assault have returned. However, in those moments, I have once again prayed and asked the Lord to bless her, and instantly the pain and hurt have gone.

"I praise the Lord for the deliverance in my life that has come through the power of a spoken blessing."

WHEN THE OPPORTUNITY IS GONE

Many people have testified to overcoming years of bitterness that began from being "cursed" or abused during childhood by a parent or other adult and finally was erased by bestowing a blessing on the offender.

But what about situations where the person who afflicted us in childhood is no longer alive—and on whom we no longer have the opportunity, therefore, to personally bestow a blessing?

In these cases, *keep blessing God!* Bless Him for the difficult experiences with that person and for how He intends to teach you and refine you through them. Bless Him for the wisdom He will give you, knowing that He allowed these circumstances in your life in His timing and for His purposes. Bless Him that He will turn your pain into a tenderness and sensitivity toward others. Bless His name! That's what Job did. He didn't bless his sorrow and loss, and he didn't bless Satan for striking his life and his family. But even in the moments of His deepest devastation, he said, "Blessed be the name of the LORD."[78]

Joseph, too, came to see beyond his harsh treatment

and painful memories to a greater good and a greater purpose. He told his repentant brothers, through tears, "As for you, you meant evil against me; but God meant it for good, in order to bring it about as it is to this day, to save many people alive."[79] And so it is for all who belong to God. He will never waste our pain, and as we daily place our trust in Him, He will shape us to look more and more like Jesus.

MAKE THE DECISION

Most likely as you've read this chapter, God has brought to mind someone who to some degree has been an "enemy" to you or to someone you love. Think carefully through the guidelines mentioned in this chapter, and consider how they fit with the other things you've learned in this book. In private prayer before God, speak aloud words of blessing upon this person. And consider how God would have you actually speak those same words directly to this person when the time is right.

🍃

BLESSING GOD

It's staggering to think that the One "from whom all bless-ings flow" also gives us the ability to bless *Him*. Yet blessing Him is something He commands us to do.

In fact, it is the very purpose for which we were created.

Blessing God is one of the strongest and most mean-ingful ways to worship and praise Him. It's not surprising that David takes the lead for us in this: "Every day I will bless You," he tells the Lord, "and I will praise Your name forever and ever."[80]

Look at all the reasons David finds for blessing his God:

- "I will bless the LORD who has given me counsel."
- "Blessed be the LORD my Rock, who trains my hands for war, and my fingers for battle."

- "Blessed be the LORD, because He has heard the voice of my supplications!"
- "Blessed be the LORD, for He has shown me His marvelous kindness in a strong city!"
- "Blessed be the Lord, who daily loads us with benefits."
- "The God of Israel is He who gives strength and power to His people. Blessed be God!"
- "The Lord lives! Blessed be my Rock! Let the God of my salvation be exalted."[81]

And what about when we don't see God doing good things for us? What about when things are going badly? In that case, there's no better example for us than that of Job. Satan was sure that Job could be made to curse God to his face.[82] But when he had lost not only his substantial wealth but all his children as well, Job still "fell to the ground and worshiped. And he said: 'Naked I came from my mother's womb, and naked shall I return there. The LORD gave, and the LORD has taken away; *blessed be the name of the LORD.*'"[83]

At the end of history, as unbelievers experience the horror of the earth being destroyed all around them in God's final outpouring of wrath against sinful humanity, they'll be cursing God more than ever.[84] But as His redeemed and chosen people, it's our privilege to bless God both now in this world and throughout the ages to come.

Our ability to bless others flows most freely when we can say with David, "I will bless the LORD at all times; His praise shall continually be in my mouth."[85]

BLESSING HIS NAME

There's nothing more worthy of our blessing than the matchless name of the Lord and all that it represents—His total nature and character. There's also no greater concern on the Lord's heart than to have His name honored.

We bless His name when from a genuine heart we tell Him, as Jesus taught us, "Hallowed be Your name." And as Daniel did when God revealed to him the content of the king's dream, we can bless the Lord's name while also praising Him for who He is and what He does:

> Blessed be the name of God forever and ever,
>> For wisdom and might are His.
> And He changes the times and the seasons;
>> He removes kings and raises up kings;
> He gives wisdom to the wise
>> And knowledge to those who have understanding.
> He reveals deep and secret things;
>> He knows what is in the darkness,
> And light dwells with Him.[86]

David knew that God's name is "exalted above all things,"[87] so he made this commitment to God: "I will bless Your name forever and ever."[88] And he gave his own heart this counsel: "Bless the LORD, O my soul; And all that is within me, bless His holy name!"[89] God wants us to bless Him with our total being and to never stop doing it.

David's final word in the book of Psalms is this counsel to everyone in all creation: "Let all flesh bless his holy name forever and ever."[90]

MAKE THE DECISION

Do you have a greater understanding now of what "blessing God" is all about and what it can accomplish? Take time now to do exactly that: Bless the Lord your God with all your heart and soul and mind and strength.

Times of testing and trial are on the horizon in your life (even more severe than what you may be facing now). When they come, will you know how to bless Him even in such difficult circumstances and not to revert to bitterness or complaining? Speak with God now about this. Ask Him to prepare you to be faithful.

Take a moment also to look back over the brief "Make the Decision" sections at the end of each chapter. Is there any unfinished business you need to quickly tend to as a result of commitments you made to yourself and to God?

Most importantly, take time to specifically thank the Lord for how He will use you in the lives of others by speaking to them His words of blessing.

A TESTIMONY

Phil and Teresa Apple, from Raleigh, North Carolina,
describe how the power of spoken blessings
produced dramatic results in their family.

My wife Teresa had suffered from chronic, unrelenting chest, back, and esophagus pain for over two and a half years, leaving her unable to sleep more than a couple of hours a night.

Doctors ran batteries of diagnostic tests, endoscopies, scans, and blood tests. Specialists inserted tubes into her esophagus, and even removed her gall bladder. But the pain never relented.

Other doctors prescribed a seemingly endless stream of acid blockers. Eventually we had exhausted over a dozen new drugs costing thousands of dollars. None was remotely successful. Finally, Teresa was told that this was all psycho-somatic—"just in her head"—and that she needed antide-pressants.

As the pain went on and on, Teresa began to believe she had an undiscovered cancer that would soon take her home.

We realize now that this all began with a family tragedy. My dad, Teresa's real father figure, was brutally assaulted with a hammer in a robbery attempt in North Carolina, leaving him in a coma with severe brain damage.

It was 1995, and we lived in Florida. Teresa was four months pregnant. Since I'm an only child, the responsibility to care for Dad fell on me. When I finally had to return to work in Florida, Teresa stayed at Dad's side in North Carolina.

During this time, the men responsible for the crime were arrested and convicted, neither expressing a word of remorse.

With some difficulty, I obtained a job transfer to North Carolina to better care for Dad. We moved in December of 2000, but Dad died in January of 2001. The reason for our move was gone. My wife had left her church support group of fourteen years in Florida. Soon after, the pains began.

After over two and a half years, we began to hear about a new Total Health program in Nashville. We signed up as soon as finances and schedules enabled us both to attend, in June of 2004.

We were ecstatic to learn that Bill Gothard himself would be there. On the first full day, Mr. Gothard joined us at our breakfast table. Almost immediately, he looked across the table at Teresa and asked how she was doing. That opened the floodgates!

Seeing the tears flowing from Teresa's eyes as she described the attack upon her father-in-law, Mr. Gothard told her, "You have a deep hurt. It's like a poison eating away at your system." He then explained that the only way to neutralize this venom was to verbally bless the assailant and everyone else involved in the incident. He assured her that the positive power of the verbal blessing would neutralize the toxic damage of the bitterness she was experiencing. Next, he said that she must fully forgive those who had deeply hurt her. And finally, she must thank God for allowing these things to happen and begin to list benefits that God intended to come from it.

Eager to follow these biblical steps, Teresa took my hand and prayed as her tears flowed. Following her prayer, Mr. Gothard prayed for God to bring healing to her physical body, using a believer's spiritual authority over Satan.

Almost immediately, Teresa's countenance changed. Within the hour her pains were totally gone. By that evening she did not need any of the fifteen medications that she had been taking at each meal.

The next day, she joyfully reported to the whole group how God had healed her, and how for the first time in two and a half years she was pain free.

Appendix

BIBLE PASSAGES FOR WORDS OF BLESSING

Here is a helpful list of prayer-related passages in the New Testament that especially lend themselves to being adapted as a blessing upon others.

Romans 15:5–6   2 Corinthians 1:3–7

Romans 15:13   2 Corinthians 2:14

1 Corinthians 1:4–9   2 Corinthians 13:7–9

1 Corinthians 16:23   Galatians 6:18

Ephesians 1:3–10	1 Thessalonians 5:28
Ephesians 1:15–23	2 Thessalonians 1:11–12
Ephesians 3:14–21	2 Thessalonians 2:16–17
Ephesians 6:19–20	2 Thessalonians 3:5
Ephesians 6:23–24	2 Thessalonians 3:16
Philippians 1:3–6	1 Timothy 1:12
Philippians 1:9–11	2 Timothy 4:22
Philippians 4:6–8	Philemon 1:4–7
Philippians 4:23	Hebrews 13:20–21
Colossians 1:3–6	1 Peter 1:3–9
Colossians 1:9–14	1 Peter 5:10–11
Colossians 4:2–4	2 Peter 1:2–4
1 Thessalonians 1:2–3	2 Peter 3:18
1 Thessalonians 3:12–13	2 John 1:3
1 Thessalonians 5:23–24	3 John 1:2–3

NOTES

1. Romans 12:14, 19
2. Luke 2:22–35
3. Luke 2:33
4. Luke 2:26
5. 1 Timothy 1:11
6. 1 Timothy 6:15, ESV
7. Romans 1:25
8. Isaiah 44:3, ESV
9. Acts 10:38
10. Luke 24:50–51, ESV
11. Psalm 45:2
12. John 1:14
13. John 1:16, ESV
14. Ephesians 1:3
15. Proverbs 12:25
16. Proverbs 16:24
17. Proverbs 18:21
18. James 3:6, 8–10
19. Luke 6:45
20. John 1:1
21. Ephesians 4:29, ESV
22. 2 Corinthians 5:16
23. 2 Corinthians 5:16, NLT
24. 2 Corinthians 5:16, AMP
25. Ephesians 2:10
26. 1 Peter 2:5
27. Numbers 6:24–26
28. 2 Timothy 1:7
29. 1 John 4:18
30. Philippians 4:6–7
31. 2 Corinthians 1:3
32. 1 Peter 5:10

33. Romans 15:5–7
34. Romans 15:29, ESV
35. Revelation 1:5–6
36. 1 Peter 2:9
37. Genesis 1:27–28
38. 1 Chronicles 4:10
39. 1 Chronicles 4:10
40. John 17:15
41. Jude 1:24
42. Psalm 91:11
43. 1 John 1:5
44. 2 Corinthians 4:6, ESV
45. Malachi 4:2
46. John 1:9
47. Ephesians 4:29
48. Romans 14:17
49. Romans 8:6, ESV
50. Ephesians 2:14
51. Colossians 1:20, ESV
52. John 14:27
53. Philippians 4:7
54. Numbers 6:27
55. Psalm 44:5; 54:1; 124:8
56. Psalm 148:13
57. Psalm 8:9
58. Exodus 3:14
59. Revelation 14:1
60. Proverbs 18:10
61. Matthew 10:8
62. 2 Samuel 13:25
63. Hebrews 11:20–21
64. Ephesians 5:19
65. Mark 10:16
66. James 3:8
67. Romans 12:14
68. Matthew 5:43–44
69. Romans 12:19–21
70. 1 Corinthians 5:11
71. 1 Corinthians 6:10
72. Matthew 27:44
73. Luke 23:34
74. 1 Peter 2:23, ESV
75. 1 Peter 2:21
76. 1 Peter 3:9, ESV
77. 1 Corinthians 4:12
78. Job 1:21
79. Genesis 50:20
80. Psalm 145:2
81. Psalm 16:7; 144:1; 28:6; 31:21; 68:19; 68:35; 18:46
82. Job 1:11
83. Job 1:20–21
84. Revelation 16
85. Psalm 34:1
86. Daniel 2:20–22
87. Psalm 138:2, ESV
88. Psalm 145:1
89. Psalm 103:1
90. Psalm 145:21, ESV

"The LORD, whose name is Jealous, is a jealous God."

—Exodus 34:14

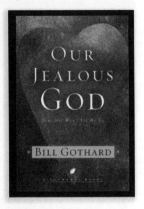

WHEN JEALOUSY IS RIGHT!

Find out why His Jealousy is your highest honor—and the pathway to unimagined blessings.

OUR JEALOUS GOD
Love That Won't Let Me Go
1-59052-225-7

HE WANTS YOUR HEART AND VOICE!

God doesn't miss a single sigh that escapes our lips. But historically, God's people most often cried out in spoken words that sprang from the depths of their being! God heard their petitions…and shook their worlds.

THE POWER OF CRYING OUT
When Prayer Becomes Mighty
1-59052-037-8

The Story Behind
The Power of Spoken Blessings

It was only a few years ago that I discovered the biblical requirement for being a true disciple of the Lord Jesus Christ. It is explained in the great commission: *"Teaching them to observe all things whatsoever I have commanded you"* (Matthew 28:20).

I began to list all the general commands Jesus gave, along with the incredible rewards He promises to those who keep them before their eyes.

- God will reveal Himself to us. (John 14:21)
- We will receive God's love. (John 15:10)
- We will know we love God. (I John 2:3, 5)
- Our prayers will be answered. (I John 3:22)
- God will dwell in us. (John 14:23)
- We will love others. (I John 5:2)
- Christ will be our friend. (John 15:14)
- We will be His disciples. (John 13:34–35)

Studying each command has opened up a whole new dimension of understanding and intimacy with Christ!

The book you are holding is based on the command to "Bless your enemies." Resources on all forty-nine general commands of Christ can be ordered on-line at store.iblp.org or by calling 800-398-1290.

Recommended Resources for Further Stud

Commands of Christ, Series 1–7, Study Books

The Commands of Christ series is a set of seven study books focusing on forty general commands Jesus gave.

The books may be used in a group setting or as a personal study. Each l includes an in-depth commentary, study questions, related names of God, a acter quality and songs that amplify the command, questions and commitmen personal application, and a journal page for recording your own insights progress as you incorporate Christ's commands into your life.

Commands of Christ Study Books 1–7, $10 ea./$7 ea. when purchased as a se

Commands of Christ Memorization and Meditation Tools Set ⎯⎯⎯⎯⎯

Designed to help you reach the goals of being a disciple of Jesus and experiencing rich fellowship with Him, this journal provides structure for an in-depth personal study of the commands of Christ and comes with a quick reference pocket guide and Scripture memory cards.

Commands of Christ Memorization and Meditation Tools Set ....

The Power for True Success ⎯⎯⎯⎯⎯

This full-color, display-quality book provides an exte study on forty-nine character qualities complete with tical definitions, biblical word studies, illustrations, analogies, historical quotes, and practical steps for dev ing godly character and achieving true success.

The Power for True Success ....

BIG CHANGE

STOP DATING THE CHURCH!
Fall in Love with the Family of God
JOSHUA HARRIS ISBN 1-59052-365-2

THE POWER OF SPOKEN BLESSINGS
BILL GOTHARD ISBN 1-59052-375-X

CHRIST OUR MEDIATOR
Finding Passion at the Cross
C. J. MAHANEY ISBN 1-59052-364-4

THE FINAL QUESTION OF JESUS
How You Can Live the Answer Today
JOE STOWELL ISBN 1-59052-204-4

WHAT'S SO SPIRITUAL ABOUT YOUR GIFTS?
HENRY & MEL BLACKABY
ISBN 1-59052-344-X

WHAT'S SO SPIRITUAL ABOUT YOUR GIFTS?
WORKBOOK
HENRY & MEL BLACKABY
ISBN 1-59052-345-8

GOD IS MORE THAN ENOUGH
TONY EVANS ISBN 1-59052-337-7

AFTER YOU'VE BLOWN IT
Reconnecting with God and Others
ERWIN LUTZER ISBN 1-59052-334-2

THE PRAYER MATRIX
Plugging in to the Unseen Reality
DAVID JEREMIAH ISBN 1-59052-181-1

TRUE FREEDOM
The Liberating Power of Prayer
OLIVER NORTH & BRIAN SMITH
ISBN 1-59052-363-6

HOW GOOD IS GOOD ENOUGH?
ANDY STANLEY ISBN 1-59052-274-5

A LITTLE POT OF OIL
A Life Overflowing
JILL BRISCOE ISBN 1-59052-234-6

OUR JEALOUS GOD
Love That Won't Let Me Go
BILL GOTHARD ISBN 1-59052-225-7

GOD IS UP TO SOMETHING GREAT
Turning Your Yesterdays into
Better Tomorrows
TONY EVANS ISBN 1-59052-038-6

PRESSURE PROOF YOUR MARRIAGE
Family First Series, #3
DENNIS & BARBARA RAINEY
ISBN 1-59052-211-7

IN THE SECRET PLACE
For God and You Alone
J. OTIS LEDBETTER ISBN 1-59052-252-4

THE PURITY PRINCIPLE
God's Safeguards for Life's Dangerous Trails
RANDY ALCORN ISBN 1-59052-195-1

SMALL BOOKS
BIG CHANGE

BIG CHANGE

A PRAYER THAT MOVES HEAVEN
Comfort and Hope for Life's Most
Difficult Moments
RON MEHL ISBN 1-57673-885-X

GROWING A SPIRITUALLY STRONG FAMILY
DENNIS & BARBARA RAINEY
ISBN 1-57673-778-0

THE TREASURE PRINCIPLE
Discovering the Secret of Joyful Giving
RANDY ALCORN ISBN 1-59052-508-6

THE TREASURE PRINCIPLE BIBLE STUDY
BRIAN SMITH & RANDY ALCORN
ISBN 1-59052-620-0

SECRETS OF THE VINE
Breaking Through to Abundance
BRUCE WILKINSON 1-57673-975-9

SECRETS OF THE VINE FOR WOMEN
DARLENE MARIE WILKINSON
ISBN 1-59052-156-0

THE PRAYER OF JABEZ
Breaking Through to the Blessed Life
BRUCE WILKINSON ISBN 1-59052-475-6

THE PRAYER OF JABEZ FOR WOMEN
DARLENE MARIE WILKINSON
ISBN 1-57673-962-7

**For a complete list of Big Change titles,
visit our website at www.bigchangemoments.com**

SMALL BOOKS
BIG CHANGE